Action Learning for Managers

Mike Pedler

in association with

the **Learning Company Project**

Published in Great Britain 1996 by Lemos & Crane
20 Pond Square
Highgate
London N6 6BA
Telephone 0181 348 8263

in association with

The Learning Company Project
28 Woodholm Road
Sheffield S11 9HT
Telephone 0114 262 1832

ISBN 1-898001-28-6

A CIP catalogue record for this book is available from the
British Library.

Cover design by Richard Newport
Text design and formatting by The Design Works, Reading
Printed by Biddles, Guildford

Contents

Acknowledgements

I acknowledge the contribution of many people in creating the ideas and materials which form this book. As an exciting method for management and organisational development, Action Learning has been worked on over the last 20 years by many creative people to produce the methodology which we work with today.

Chief of all these is Reg Revans, founder of the idea, who has contributed much to our notions of what organisational learning might be. To his particular genius and persistence goes the main credit.

This book also owes much to work which I did with John Boutall and others in producing *Action Learning for Change* for the National Health Service Training Directorate in 1992. As Action Learning is one of the main methods for working towards the Learning Company, I subsequently produced two years later a workbook for the individuals and organisations working with the Learning Company Project which appeared as *Action Learning* (Learning Company Guides: No 1).

Introduction

Action Learning is a method of problem solving and learning in groups to bring about change for individuals, teams and organisations. It works to build the relationships which help any organisation improve existing operations and learn and innovate for the future. Action Learning is perhaps the most important form of management development to emerge in the past 20 years.

As a way of working and living, Action Learning is a vital aspect of the learning company. Essentially a simple idea, Action Learning requires commitment and care to put into practice.

Action Learning for Managers is designed to:
- provide a practical introduction to Action Learning that is friendly, lively and encouraging

- help managers and professionals think through the issues they face and show how Action Learning ideas might help them
- offer managers practical advice about how to promote Action Learning in their organisation
- provide one route to implementing learning company* strategies.

How to use this book

The guidance in this book is structured around nine key questions – 'What is Action Learning?', 'Will it work in my organisation?', 'What does an Action Learning programme look like?', 'How does an Action Learning set work?', 'What is an Action Learning problem?', 'What skills are developed in Action Learning?', 'How do you evaluate Action Learning?', 'Surely Action Learning can't do everything?', and 'Where can I get more information?'.

Each question forms the basis for a chapter which contains three elements:

1 *an explanation* – a response to the title question

2 *a case example* – to illustrate the explanation

3 *a resource* – a questionnaire or checklist, for instance, to help with Action Learning activities.

---

* The learning company is a vision of what an ambitious organisation could aim for. A learning company facilitates the learning of all its people and is able consciously to transform itself as a whole. (See M Pedler, J Burgoyne and T Boydell *The Learning Company: a strategy for sustainable growth* McGraw-Hill, 1991). I use the word 'company' not to designate any legal or commercial status, but in the old sense of a group of people engaged in a joint enterprise or task.

1 What is Action Learning?

In some ways this first question is the most difficult. Reg Revans never gives a one sentence definition and has always maintained that there is no one form or version of Action Learning. Although the idea may be essentially simple, it is concerned with profound knowledge of oneself and the world, and cannot be communicated as a formula or technique. Given this proviso, it is possible to describe Action Learning as it is currently applied in many organisations today.

Action Learning is a method for individual and organisational development. Working in small groups, people tackle important organisational issues or problems and learn from their attempts to change things.

Action Learning has four elements:

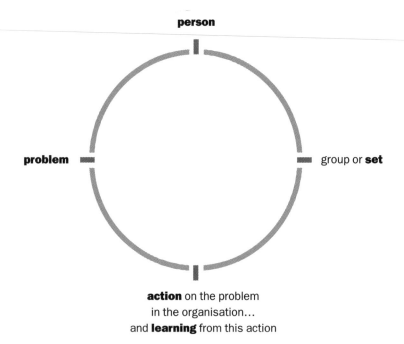

person

problem

group or **set**

action on the problem
in the organisation…
and **learning** from this action

Action Learning brings people together to exchange, support and challenge each other in seeking to act and learn. So:

first, each person joins and takes part voluntarily. You can't be sent or send anyone else (though you might work hard at persuading people!)

second, each person must own a managerial or organisational problem on which they want to act

third, because we need friends in such circumstances, sets or groups of action learners meet to help each other think through the issues, create options, and above all…

fourth, …take action and learn from the effects of that action.

One of the main premises of Action Learning is that learning and action require each other. In Revans' words:

'there is no learning without action and no (sober and deliberate) action without learning'.

There are many small group meetings in organisations which resemble Action Learning. 'Self-help groups', 'support groups', 'learning sets', 'self-development groups', 'productivity improvement meetings', 'quality circles' and so on may all well be doing Action Learning. It doesn't matter what a group is called; the acid test is whether people in that group are there to get support, challenge and encouragement to take action on their organisational problems and to learn from this.

This is one of its strengths. Because Action Learning is both profound and simple it is never in danger, as mere techniques are, of being here today and gone tomorrow. We always need to re-invent our own ways of putting the basic ideas into practice. This inventing element is what maintains the life in Action Learning.

It's as simple – and as hard – as that. The only certain way to get a taste for what Action Learning is like is to do it. However you can get a better idea of what is involved in Action Learning from listening to others engaged in action and learning. Here is a **case example** which gives a flavour of life in a set meeting:

An Action Learning set of doctors and managers have been meeting together in a hospital. Donald, a consultant physician, has taken as his problem the degree of stress experienced by nurses and other medical staff in his unit. Here other members are questioning him about the problem and also wanting to know what has happened since their last meeting:

Donald Well, it's worse than I thought – our length of stay figures are too high, and the turnover interval is down to less than a day – no wonder everyone rushes around like headless chickens. Morale is low, sickness and absence is way up amongst the nurses and the standard of care is generally too low.

Shamilla It sounds awful, but what about the other figures you were going to bring after the last meeting… you know, about the types of admissions, the case mix and so on?

Donald Ah well… yes… this is a bit embarrassing. When I looked at admissions it seems that my senior colleague has far more electives than anyone else – about 40% compared with 10% elsewhere.

Paul So… what do you make of that?

Val 'Research' of course – what else!

Donald Er... yes, probably.

Shamilla So, what can you do about it then, Donald?

A discussion follows about possible options for action. At the same time Donald is getting a lot of support from his set, who are well aware that this is a delicate situation. No one tells Donald what to do:

Donald (tentatively) I could publish my figures at the next audit meeting...?

Lawrence What effect would that have?

Donald Well, he might start to argue, but more likely he would just walk out and say my figures are rubbish and I don't know what I'm talking about...

Paul What else could you do? Who else would like to see this issue tackled?

Donald Well, the Chief Executive wants it badly, but... well, frankly I doubt if she'd back me up if it came to it...

Lawrence Have you asked her?

Donald Well no ... but you know how it is ...

Lawrence OK I can see the problem... but... until you ask...?

> **Eventually, after several more rounds of suggestions and questions Donald decides he will try talking to his senior colleague in private. He'll do this before the next meeting and bring back the results. He looks nervous as he says this. Donald having had his turn, the set then turns its attention to Shamilla...**

Taking action in organisations – action of the 'sober and deliberate' sort – is often not easy. It may require us to do something different – to 'fit out' rather than fit in. There is risk involved in learning in this way; sometimes of incuring the wrath of others, but more often with risking some aspect of ourselves – our reputation or self-image. The learning from such risks can be profound, and the support and challenge of others is important in such circumstances.

Finally in this chapter here is a **resource** which gives a more formal definition of Action Learning and which could be used as a handout.

What is Action Learning?

Action Learning was developed by Reg Revans as the best way to educate managers. It is based on his premise that:

'There can be no learning without action and no (sober and deliberate) action without learning.'

Revans suggests that organisations (and the individuals in them) cannot flourish unless their rate of learning (**L**) is equal to or greater than, the rate of change (**C**) being experienced: $L \geq C$.

Learning has two elements – traditional instruction or **programmed knowledge**, and critical reflection or **questioning insight**. This gives the learning equation: $L = P + Q$.

He also distinguishes between puzzles and problems. Puzzles have 'best' solutions and can be solved via the application of programmed knowledge with the help of experts. Problems have no right answers and are tackled by people in different ways by the exercise of questioning insight. Programmed knowledge can be helpful but it should only be sought after careful reflection on what knowledge is needed and why.

Action Learning sets (or groups) bring people together in order to:

■ work on and through hitherto intractable problems of managing and organising. This must be a voluntary commitment

■ work on problems which personally engage the set members – situations in which 'I am part of the problem and the problem is part of me'

■ check individual perceptions of the problem, to clarify and render it more manageable, and to create and explore alternatives for action

■ take action in the light of new insight. This insight begins to change the situation. An account of the effects of the action are brought back to the set for further shared reflection and exploration

■ provide the balance of support and challenge (warmth and light) which will enable each member to act and learn effectively

■ be aware of group processes and develop effective teamwork. Usually sets have an adviser or facilitator whose role is to help members identify and acquire the skills of action and learning

■ focus on learning at three levels:

1 about the problem which is being tackled

2 about what is being learned about oneself

3 about the process of learning itself, i.e. 'learning to learn'.

The second and third levels are essential for the transfer of learning to other situations.

(Adapted from the original by Kath Aspinwall)

Although resources like this one can be helpful in introducing and explaining the idea to people, it is often best to do this quickly and then set up a small trial or experiment in Action Learning to give more of an experience. You can't really teach what Action Learning is; but you can provide the situations in which others can learn through action.

Some ideas for doing this are given later in the book, but at this point, you might be wondering, 'If this apparently simple method is so profound and powerful, will it work in my organisation?'

② Will it work in my organisation?

'Doubt ascending speeds wisdom from above' (R W Revans)

In organisational terms this means that good questions from people actually help senior managers to make good decisions. This is a nice idea. However as someone once said 'In my company, doubt ascending speeds *retribution* from above!'.

So, the first question is – *what sort of organisation is yours?*

Are questions likely to speed wisdom from above or to deposit retribution on those below? In many organisations, the questioning of senior management decisions is frowned upon or simply not done. People see it as a 'career limiting' thing to do. Actually of course, it is a sign of confidence and faith in your own ability. In oppressive organisations only the brave and/or foolish are up to it, but in organisations which seek to build up the abilities and confidence of all their people it is a sign of health and fitness. However it is difficult where there is no tradition of participation in decisions.

In a very efficient, family-owned retail department store, the Managing Director was singing the praises of his monthly management meeting to a visitor. A visiting manager asked: 'When were you last questioned on some aspect of company policy?'. The MD looked astonished: 'I can't remember that ever happening', he said. Neither could he see why this might be a desirable thing to happen in the future.

One of the main contributions of Action Learning is the creation of a culture of enquiry and questioning – an essential aspect of the learning climate needed in the learning company.

The second question is – *is this what you and your colleagues want?*

Some organisations do survive and even prosper with one-way, top-down communications; but those beset by rapid environmental change and increasing competition for markets or resources may find that these constitute serious 'learning disabilities' on the part of the organisation. As W Edwards Deming once famously said 'survival is not compulsory'.

In deciding whether Action Learning will work in your organisation, consider the following:

Is there a readiness for Action Learning?

Does the idea fit with the current stage of development of the organisation? Are people ready to be encouraged to take more initiatives, have more of a say, be entrepreneurial, take risks, run their jobs as if they were their own small businesses? Action Learning will not work for the organisation if things are going in the opposite direction.[†]

Do you really want to do Action Learning?

It is not for everyone at all times. Organisations which do lots of training do not necessarily provide the right welcome for Action Learning. Action Learning requires significant organisational problems to work with and people willing to have a go at action and learning with all the implications of these. It needs energy to set up – have you got enough for this at the moment?

[†] Although it might work very well for individuals who can find some space and freedom in the oasis of a set. A friend, who was once the management development manager in a large family-owned and 'feudal' organisation, used to organise – unknown to his superiors – sets of people who were fed up with the company. At the first meeting in one set of six, all those present said that they wanted to get out and asked if the set could help them with their escape plans. After eight or so meetings, two had indeed left but the other four had worked on ways of improving their working lives, by moving departments, finding projects and new friends or allies. All this happened in the 'shadow side' of the organisation – unknown to and unsanctioned by senior managers.

Is there support and commitment from the top?

Despite the story of the 'feudal company' above, as well as good problems/issues and willing participants, Action Learning is likely to have the biggest impact on individuals and on the organisation when it has support from powerful people.

Can Action Learning support their vision and aims for the organisation?

Does it offer a way forwards on some of *their* problems?

Are they able to give a welcome to the questioning of current practices, to change efforts and experiments?

The following **case example** shows what Action Learning can do in a company where this sort of readiness and commitment from the top is apparent:

case example

Action Learning in John Tann Security Ltd

Colin, John, Les and Pete, four line managers from John Tann Security Ltd, a heavy metal fabrication company which makes safes, vaults and security equipment, formed a management action group with the help of an outside adviser, Norman Brown.

The company was faced with a number of problems including small batches, high product variety and changing fashions in the market for security equipment. The directors of John Tann wanted to increase output and efficiency and also develop the management potential of their key people. Unusually perhaps, the directors also felt that 'often good ideas in a company do not originate at Board level but are the brain children of senior management'. They wanted to establish an environment in which 'ideas would flow upwards through the company structure'.

The four managers met weekly over a six-month period with the external adviser and developed well as a group. Another unusual feature of this group is that they reviewed their success not only at the end of this period but also – all of them still working in the company and together with their sponsoring director – four years later. They evaluated the benefits under four headings:

1 **Productivity** – the original target was to increase this by 15% and taking year one as zero, the figures for the four years were +11%, +19%, +17% and +13%. No one claims that this improvement stems entirely from the Action Learning – but it is seen as the major factor.

2 **Individual Management Development** – the participants believe that their Action Learning experience 'was the most significant factor' in establishing better decision making, more delegation, less defensive attitudes and improved ability to take criticism, improved self-confidence and leadership, proper application of disciplinary procedures and the ability to confide in their director in the belief that 'he wanted them to manage and would allow them to do so'.

3 **Team building** – they now operate as a much more effective team.

4 **Continuing use of Action Learning** – the four formed a set for their deputies and shared the role of adviser in order to pass on what they had learned. Although this set met for several meetings it petered out. They felt this was due to the absence of an external adviser and the presence of one of themselves as part of the company hierarchy.

Based on Norman Brown 'Improving Management Morale and Efficiency' in M Pedler (Ed.) Action Learning in Practice *2nd ed. (Gower, 1991) pp 135–146.*

John Tann is perhaps the ideal setting for Action Learning. The participants are all keen to have a go, the problems are tangible and important and there is support from the top. There is also another important factor at work here – the directors have the unusual and refreshing belief that the best ideas do not come from them but from those beneath them – and they recognise the value of getting a flow of ideas upwards. Whilst there are plenty of directors who say they want this, it is unusual to find leaders able to 'give the power away' and take the risks inherent in this position.

Finally in this chapter a **resource** – a questionnaire for you to test your organisational readiness for Action Learning:

resource

Questionnaire:

Organisational readiness for Action Learning

This will help you assess the chance of Action Learning working in your company. For each statement score the company from 1 (not much like us) to 5 (very like us).

In this organisation...

... people are rewarded for asking good questions	1	2	3	4	5
... people often come up with new ideas	1	2	3	4	5
... there is a fairly free flow of communications	1	2	3	4	5
... conflict is surfaced and dealt with rather than suppressed	1	2	3	4	5
... we are encouraged to learn new skills	1	2	3	4	5
... we take time out to reflect on experiences	1	2	3	4	5
... there are plenty of books, films, packages and other resources for learning	1	2	3	4	5
... people help, encourage and constructively criticise each other	1	2	3	4	5

... we are flexible in our working

patterns and used to working

on several jobs at once   1   2   3   4   5

... senior people never pull rank

and always encourage others

to speak their minds   1   2   3   4   5

Now total up your score. If you scored...

... between   Action Learning probably won't work
10 and 20   in your organisation until things open
                     up a bit more

... 21 to 40   Yes – Action Learning should work
                     well to help you achieve your
                     purposes

... over 40   You don't need Action Learning – or...
                     maybe Action Learning would help to
                     develop your critical faculties?

Organisational readiness means being in that situation where Action Learning offers sufficient challenge to the existing order, yet where there is enough openness and support to give it a chance to thrive.

There are some companies, especially young pioneer organisations, where the learning is so uninhibited, so natural and so everyday, that relationships between people are like those of the colleagues in the Action Learning set. People share problems as soon as they perceive them, they offer help readily and without embarrassment, everybody puts their shoulders to the wheel when necessary and so on. As organisations get bigger, older, more systematised, they can lose this natural learning ability. Action Learning is a principal way of loosening and shaking in these settings.

So, having decided whether Action Learning is right for your organisation, what does an Action Learning programme look like?

③ What does an Action Learning programme look like?

As was said at the outset, there is no single, correct form for Action Learning. A group of people may meet together at their own instigation or a company may set up a large programme with many groups and a complicated structure of inter-communications. This larger, organisational programme will probably have at least four main structural components:

Sets...

... groups of people who work by *meeting* for a full or half day, every two to six weeks, over several months. With the help of a facilitator or adviser sets can decide how many meetings to have, where, for how long, when to stop, to evaluate and so on. This self-management is a first step in people taking responsibility for their own actions and learning.

Sets need *regular members* who try hard to attend all meetings which focus on members' *problems or tasks* – the vehicles for action and learning which form the agenda for the set.

Sponsors...

... who support members in tackling their problems in the organisation and who help with evaluation of outcomes. Sometimes these are the members' line managers, but ideally they are 'off line' senior people willing to act as mentors and give time to the personal and professional development of those involved.

Sponsors may act in a specific project-focused way or as mentors with a broader career or life-centred focus.

Some programmes offer mentoring as a separate and additional opportunity. It is important not to clutter the programme with various roles or to offer too much.

Advisers...

... or facilitators who help the set get started, encourage people to share ideas and concerns with each other, and facilitate the development of the set as a powerful learning system.

The adviser is mainly concerned with learning processes in the set and with making these explicit. This helps the set members understand better how they, and other people, learn. Of particular importance are the balancing of support and challenge which each person needs at particular times, and helping the members of the set to reflect on their learning.

Sets can work without advisers where members ensure that these learning process tasks are accomplished –

either by taking it in turn to act as facilitator or by their general level of skill and awareness. However, there are limits to this, no member can put themselves outside the set in the same way as can an adviser.

Conferences...

... are a good way of linking the Action Learning sets with the whole organisation – thereby increasing the likelihood of organisational learning. With more than one set these are an opportunity to get together, often with senior people, to report on action and learning. A conference can be used to start off a programme, and also be a good place to finish.

case example

In Keatings, a small printing company, all 50 staff were involved in action learning groups. These sets were formed by taking people from different work processes and mixing them together in fours and fives. Each set picked a joint problem from a list of organisational issues collected by consultants, for example the design of a work process or a relationship with a customer. They were given two hours of the firm's time on a weekly basis over three months to work on these problems. At the end of that time, each set met with the owner and managing director and made presentations. If he approved their proposals (which he did in all cases but one) the group was then given the responsibility for implementing their plan. At the end of six months the managing director hosted a dinner and celebration at which he thanked people for their efforts.

The following **case example** illustrates the structure of an Action Learning programme:

Design for an Action Learning programme in a large engineering company

Reorganisation had created 36 new teams, and the team leaders took part in the programme with the help of external advisers. The problem which each team leader addressed was essentially the same 'How do I make this new job/team/structure work?'; the action and learning on the problem was unique to that person, but shared in the sets and the management conferences.

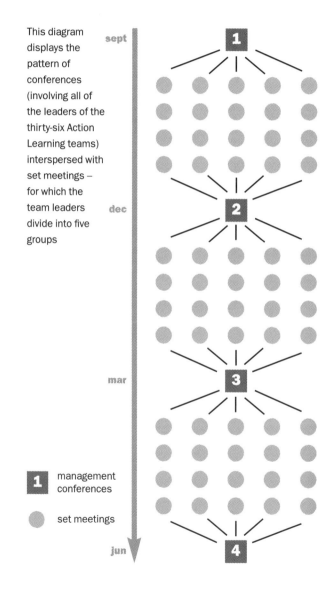

This diagram displays the pattern of conferences (involving all of the leaders of the thirty-six Action Learning teams) interspersed with set meetings – for which the team leaders divide into five groups

1 management conferences

set meetings

sept

dec

mar

jun

The start-up conference included a visit from the MD and Chairman and also an introductory activity to give people an idea of what Action Learning is like and to get them started on thinking about their 'problems'. See the **resource** below for design details of this conference.

The final conference heard evaluation reports from each set; it was followed by dinner and again involved the MD and Chairman.

The **resource** consists of a design for a start-up conference like the one used in the **case example** above. Starting well is important and it is worth giving people the opportunity to experience what it is like to work in a small group on problems brought by members, as well as having them hear from a leader about why this programme is important to the organisation.

resource

Design for a half-day start-up conference

9.00 **Welcome and introductions**
Programme manager

9.30 **Where the company is going**
Senior manager

9.50 **What is Action Learning?**
Consultant

10.10 **Activity – 'Problems and questions'**
In the whole group

10.30 **Activity – 'Working in a set'**
*Split into groups (temporary sets) and work for
an hour on some issues raised by members of
the group with the help of an adviser*

Tea/coffee taken in these groups

11.30 **Feedback and questions**
Programme manager and consultant

12.00 **Next steps**
Programme manager and consultant
Including:

   1 **Invitation to join the programme**
*Note: Action Learning only works with
volunteers who want to act and learn by
tackling a problem. It should be made as*

comfortable as possible not to join where there are good reasons e.g. personal matters or being part of a similar programme elsewhere. Being 'too busy' is not a good reason for not taking part.

2 If you decide to join – then the **next steps** are:

i to inform the programme manager

ii discuss the programme and your 'problem' with your manager, sponsor, mentor

iii prepare an initial statement of your problem as you see it.

12.30 **Close**

After this taster session you may have to do some unofficial work behind the scenes to get the Action Learning sets started. People may wish to talk through concerns, or what sort of problems they can discuss, prior to making the decision to join. Some managers may need encouraging to give their people the proper permission to take part. Do whatever it takes to get the sets off to a good start.

For example, it is worth considering whether you will allow the temporary groups which form on the day to continue if they wish to. Sometimes, if the day goes well for a particular group, they may want to get on with it. The only sensible thing to do with that sort of energy is to get out of the way.

Once started, how does an Action Learning set work?

4 How does an Action Learning set work?

At the first meeting, the adviser will encourage members to introduce themselves, to explore what they want to get from the programme and to discuss some ground rules for working together.

The first meeting will usually include each person taking some time to describe the problem or issue which they want to tackle. At this stage it may be tentative or unformed, and this is no bad thing. If a person is clear about what needs doing and what they want to do, that's fine, the set can get on and help as best they can. However a sincere question which begins with 'How can I…' is a very good starting place for action and learning.

Although all groups develop differently and create their own patterns of membership, communication and management, at subsequent meetings the following format may apply:

- *catching-up* – a session which allows each person to share immediate news and serves to re-integrate the group

- *agenda setting* – members set the agenda, decide on a 'batting order' and allocate the available time. In principle members have equal time but this may be varied depending on need, urgency and so on.

- *progress reports* – each person takes it in turn to report on progress since the last meeting and the problem as it is now. Keeping the focus on the person and their problem, questioning, supporting, challenging and offering resources of various sorts, the others help the person to learn from what has happened and to find a direction or set new goals for the following period.

- *review* – a period at the end of each session for feedback and discussion of the group process – 'What worked well?' 'What was difficult in this meeting?' 'How could we be more effective?'

It is usually a mistake to try to get down to business too early, especially if it is some time since members have been together. To be here properly, it is useful for everyone to remember what is different about this group and what was talked about last time and so on. Some of the best groups I have been in have taken special care in bringing everyone in before getting on with some very productive work in a much shorter time than you might think possible. Ten or fifteen minutes in a focused group working well together can be worth an hour in one which is not functioning as a collective team.

Some of the important processes in the set are:

● people **sharing** their perception of the problem to be tackled. This involves some self-disclosure and talking about their feelings, fears, hopes, limitations, strengths and so on and also confidential information about their units and colleagues. This means that sets need to establish...

- **ground rules** to govern behaviour inside and outside the set. An example of a rule might be that all members have an equal right to the time and attention of the set. Another might be that people cannot discuss 'set business' outside. Good ground rules help with...

- **supporting** people in their attempts at understanding, action and learning. A good set builds up over time in its ability to offer members both support and challenge to their existing views and perceptions. Warmth (or support) is often needed before light (or challenge) can be accepted. Challenge can be provided by...

- **questioning** – where each person presents their 'status report' or current understanding of their problem, whilst other members listen, express support, make suggestions, but above all pose questions. This may lead to questions which the person may not have considered for themselves. The aim is to find those questions which lead to the person *questioning themselves*. When this happens it is this process which can lead to *questioning insight* or Q (an essential part of the learning equation set out on page 20). Sets improve in their ability to both support and challenge as they mature. This takes time, regular meetings and consistent membership to develop a good…

● **set development process** whereby the set forms, matures and learns to work creatively and productively. Members, having got to know each other and perhaps tested each other out, begin to create a strong joint commitment. In a mature set there is that sense of comradeship – of being 'all for one and one for all' – where all members take pleasure and satisfaction whenever one person has a small 'victory' or when the penny drops for someone and they get a new insight into their situation. The group process is helped by regular…

● **review** in which the set stops work on problems and reflects on how well the group as a whole is working. 'How effective are we in helping each other to act and learn?' Facilitation and evaluation are key processes which must happen in any set.

The following **case example** illustrates the questioning process in an Action Learning set.

In an early meeting of a set set up as part of a management development programme in a major airline, the adviser thinks that everything is too busy, people are cutting each other off and not listening very well. She offers this view of the group process and on finding that others agree, suggests a method...

Adviser Let's start with Caroline. Can you summarise your situation in one or two sentences, Caroline? Now – everyone else, please listen, don't speak but instead write down any thoughts or questions you have.

Caroline Well, it comes down to the fact that I have agreed with my boss to try and improve relationships with some of the main suppliers to our department. The quality of some of what we get is very variable, delivery times in some cases are poor and we have more than one supplier for items such as stationery. Basically I think we have too many of them, but people are committed to their particular contacts, and because they are very individualistic it has really been up to them. I can see that we could easily rationalise things but it's important to keep good relationships all round... is that enough to start with?

Adviser Yes, I think so, thank you Caroline. Now let's see what other people made of this so far – the interesting thing about working in an Action Learning set is that you find out how differently people see things. I'd like everyone to offer Caroline a question – so if you have made an observation, perhaps you could turn it into a question – now Caroline, you are not to answer these just now, just listen and write down word for word what people say.

In two minutes the other six set members offer 19 questions, including:

How many suppliers do you have now?

Have you spoken to any suppliers?

Have you quantified the costs of poor quality, late deliveries etc?

What's the history? How long has it been like this?

You talk about what the boss wants – what do you want?

What's in it for your boss?

Who else – apart from you and the boss – thinks this is a problem?

What's your relationship like with your boss?

How do your colleagues feel about the situation?

How have your colleagues got to behave differently?

Whose side are you on?

What have you got to gain from acting on this?

Why change? What are the benefits?

Adviser Caroline, which of these questions do you want to pursue? Which of them are interesting to you?

Caroline They are all good questions, but the ones which I hadn't really thought about are Oliver's about what I want and also the one about whose side am I on... what do you mean by whose side am I on...?

The set then continues with Caroline back in charge of her time...

Of course this is just one example of how a set might work together. There are so many differences depending upon what each individual brings and on the culture or cultures of the organisations to which they belong. Some of the operational guidelines for a set are worth formalising as ground rules. The **resource** for this chapter gives of an example of ground rules for a set.

Ground rules for Action Learning

The set should establish its own ground rules and it can operate to any rules which members agree upon. Some discussion should take place at the first meeting and the resulting rules should be re-visited at the second meeting and at review sessions to check on their continuing appropriateness and effectiveness. Some of the important ground rules which many groups will share are:

■ **confidentiality** – matters discussed in the group are not to be taken outside.

Confidentiality is often first on a group's list, but what does it mean? Can I talk about *my* actions, thoughts, feelings and so on, to other people? Can I disclose this particular thing to my mentor? 'Confidentiality' needs clarification in most sets.

■ **commitment** to attending and having a really good reason if you can't

■ everyone has a right to their **time** – but they don't have to take it

■ everyone should be **listened** to

■ we agree to offer each other **support and challenge** but avoid judgments

■ it is safe here to admit **needs, weaknesses and mistakes**

■ **punctuality** – we should start and finish on time.

To stress again – each group must agree its own rules – whatever works for that group are the

right rules. Some of the other ground rules which we've seen in groups are:

- no smoking
- rotating around each person's workplace
- each meeting starts with bids for time
- at each session, part of the time is given to taking it in turn to teach something to the rest of the set
- meeting outside the set in twos and threes is OK
- the adviser should have some time in the set for his/her issues
- achievements will be celebrated in an appropriate way
- members should keep a log book of progress on their problem
- set meetings can be at members' homes.

Don't over-formalise the ground rules, they are really there to help members discuss some aspects of their working relationship from time to time.

Now, having got the set off to a good start, what about the problems which the members bring? What is a good problem?

⑤ What is an Action Learning *problem*?

One of the predictable difficulties to be had in communicating Action Learning is the use of the word 'problem'. Some find the use of this word off-putting – perhaps because they associate 'problem' with things personal, that is not for public consumption. For this reason many people use other words. I usually say something like 'a *problem* in Action Learning is an issue, a concern, an opportunity or a task which you want to do something about'.

For Revans, the problem is the starting place for enquiry and action. Until we find something to be a problem for us, there is not the engagement with the world necessary for learning. He makes the distinction between problem and puzzle. Puzzles are things which may seem like problems but in fact there is some knowledge, some solution which already exists, which will give you the answer. Unlike puzzles there are no right answers for problems, although you can take action on them to change the situation in some way.

Being unable to start my car is a problem for me, but it's really a puzzle – there is someone out there who knows how to start it; but getting my colleague to change the way he works in relation to me is a true problem in the Action Learning sense – that is a situation which is not amenable to right answers. (Though no doubt this will not stop many of us looking for them in books of the 'One Minute Manager' sort!)

In this way a good problem is a good vehicle for learning – it allows us to come up with ideas for action, to try them out and then to reflect on that action to see what we have learned about the problem itself and about ourselves, the way we think, act, and relate to others.

The problem being the primary vehicle for action and learning, it should be demanding but not overwhelming. When Action Learning takes place in a company or where people are sponsored by their companies, then the problem should address an unresolved managerial issue at job, team, departmental, inter-department or whole organisation level. We are often beset by plenty of problems, and tackling one not only moves us forwards in this particular situation, it also contributes to our learning about how we work on all problems.

The **case example** below gives some ideas about the different sorts of problem which people might work on in an Action Learning set:

An Action Learning set in Hallam City Council

The first meeting of an Action Learning Set in Hallam City Council revealed at least three different kinds of problem.

Angela's was quite focused and specific. She had a graduate trainee on a six-month attachment. She had accepted the responsibility of acting as a mentor to him but felt that he was not fitting in very well. At first she had given him the benefit of the doubt and, anyway, she was just too busy. Now she had received one or two complaints about work quality to add to the various odd comments she had heard. Angela felt she should do something about it. She was concerned that she not lived up to her promise and that she was letting down both the trainee and her department. How should she tackle the problem?

The set adviser observed that this was a very clear-cut problem which made it easy for members to focus their attention and come up with options for action. However, there could well be deeper issues underlying the apparently simple problem.

Roy's problem was different. He had been told when he joined his present department that he would be able to develop an area of work concerned with tenant participation in decisions about housing management and maintenance – in which he has a great personal and professional interest. However, since starting the job he had got precisely nowhere and he was beginning to feel that his boss was not so much not especially interested in the work as actively opposed to it. Fed up with this, Roy doesn't know whether to push on this or whether to explore other ways of making a start. He wonders aloud whether race comes into it. Roy is black, as are many of the tenants on his patch; his boss is white.

The set adviser acknowledges Roy's feelings and concerns and notes that this is a very different problem from Angela's. Action is less straightforward and hedged around with areas of sensitivity. The problem will not be easy to resolve but that there is a great potential here for 'sober and deliberate' action.

Kevan's problem is different again. His department is an unhappy place. The Chief Officer has been retired 'sick' after great pressure from Councillors who have accused him of impropriety over the use of official funds and equipment. The old Chief Officer had run the department for 28 years and everyone thought of it as his. Kevan recognised that in many ways procedures had been 'somewhat casual'. However at least everyone knew where they were under the old regime, and now all was at sea. There was the threat of a review hanging over the whole department and the old deputy – now the acting Chief Officer – was identified with the old boss. The department is under great pressure as a result of CCT (Compulsory Competitive Tendering) and is likely lose work and therefore jobs. Kevan summed it up: 'we just haven't got our act together.'

The set adviser remarks that some problems have to be made more local and specific otherwise they are just too overwhelming – not only for Kevan, but for others in the set too. She asks Kevan to describe his own small team...

These are all very different sorts of problem but they have two things in common. First, they are all amenable to action and learning; secondly they all have organisational and personal aspects. This is always the case in a problem worthy of the name. This is because the person tackling the problem must have a sense of personal ownership of it – she or he must want to do something about it and to learn from it – otherwise there will be no action and learning. The person may also have a sponsor in the company who has invested some ownership in having this problem tackled – which adds something else to the sense of personal commitment.

So there are two aspects to action and learning on a problem: **action** (which includes thinking, exploring, rehearsing and actually doing) *inside* me and *outside* on the problem in the organisation. **Learning** is similarly *both* about me *and* about the problem in the organisation:

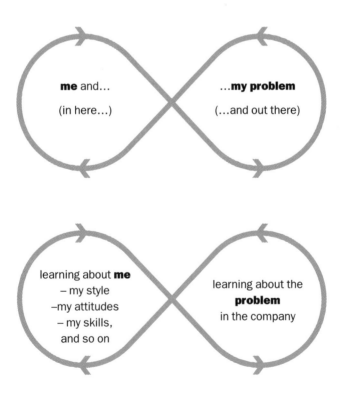

Giving it a good go

This issue of problem ownership and personal commitment is crucial. A senior manager once explained to me that he had put forward Richard, a senior and experienced shopfloor worker for a managerial Action Learning programme because 'he would give it a good go'. He did. This has been one of my 'acid tests' ever since.

The **resource** for this chapter offers some questions to help you think through a suitable problem, opportunity or issue for work in an Action Learning set.

Action Learning problem brief

Here are some questions to help you think through a suitable problem, opportunity or issue for work in an Action Learning set.

1 Describe your problem situation in one sentence:

_____

_____

_____

_____

2 Why is this important?

i To you?

_____

_____

ii To your company?

_____

_____

3 How will you recognise progress on this problem?

_____

_____

_____

4 Who else would like to see progress on this problem?

_____

_____

_____

5 What difficulties do you anticipate?

_____

_____

_____

6 What are the benefits if this problem is reduced or resolved?

i To me?

_____

_____

ii To the organisation?

_____

_____

In the John Tann example given in chapter 2, we saw that the members of the set had very clear ideas about what they wanted to see happen in the company. Sometimes it is difficult to define problems tightly enough to give good measurable outcomes or success criteria like this. Nevertheless this is not a reason for not trying.

The attempt should always be made to develop a picture or vision of how things could be different. Sometimes you can capture the difference best by asking people to draw a picture or write a short story or fable of what it would be like if it were different and better around here in this respect. People can sometimes draw or describe a picture of changed attitudes, or better relationships, or shared understanding, where defining measurable 'success criteria' is just not possible. An example of a drawing which helped can be found in chapter 8.

Having defined, and probably redefined, some good problems, what are the skills which members of a set need to demonstrate and develop?

⑥ What skills are developed in Action Learning?

Action Learning provides an opportunity to develop many valuable skills – and the practice of these helps to get the most out of it. There are three roles in the Action Learning set – each of which is develops particular skills and qualities:

1 set member (presenting your problem)

2 set member (helping others with their problems)... and...

3 facilitator.

Some of the skills and abilities which can be learned in these roles are:

Set member (presenting your problem)

- Taking and holding the focus of the set
- Presenting a problem
- Asking for help, advice, assistance
- Being able to receive – help, advice, feedback, and challenge
- Ability to reflect on what you receive and experience
- Staying in charge of your time, problem, learning
- Planning next steps
- Proactivity (a tendency to initiate action)
- Skills in organisational politics
- Resilience and perseverance
- Self-belief

Set member (helping others with their problems)

- Belief in others (in their ability to understand the

world in their way, take action on their problem etc.

- Empathy
- Credulous listening (ability to listen to others and suspend your own evaluations)
- Ability to give – help, advice, assistance
- Questioning
- Supporting
- Challenging
- Generating options for action
- Willingness to support outside the set

Facilitator

In addition to the skills and abilities of a set member (helping others):

- Understanding learning processes in individuals, groups and organisations
- Understanding the micro-politics of an organisation
- Facilitating members' giving to and receiving from each other

- Ability to summarise and draw the 'big picture'
- Ability to question oneself, admit uncertainties and errors without threatening the security of the set

These skills might be broadly defined as learning skills (although some of them are more tendencies, abilities or qualities as well as skills). The purpose of them is to help people round the action and learning cycle:

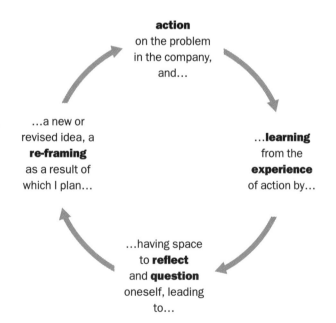

action
on the problem
in the company,
and…

…**learning**
from the
experience
of action by…

…having space
to **reflect**
and **question**
oneself, leading
to…

…a new or
revised idea, a
re-framing
as a result of
which I plan…

The **case example** below gives some examples of what people have learned from working in sets.

What individuals have learned from Action Learning

With the help of various sorts of evaluation we can form an impression of what can be learned in an Action Learning programme. The following comments, taken from various reviews, illustrates the learning – about oneself and about the organisation – which can result.

One manager learned a lot about how to make things happen:

'I knew what had to be done after a couple of sessions in the set – the problem was how to do it? I was keen but no one else seemed to be bothered. I was encouraged by the set to go around and talk to people who might be interested. For a while nothing much seemed to happen and then it was if everyone thought it was a good idea! There was actually no resistance there, it was just me, imagining it...'

One person found that she was part of the problem:

'When I joined the group I was very clear about the problem I had and I simply expected the others to give me the benefit of their experience and more or less tell

me what they thought I should do. To some extent this happened but what I hadn't expected was that I would be pushed and prodded and encouraged to really think through my problem for myself. What I learned was that this issue was as much to do with me and the way I operate as a Finance Director as it was to do with the apparent practical blockage which was bugging me, my boss and the others in the department.'

Another manager learned the valuable skill of questioning:

'You can try to teach individuals, but only they can learn... I am probably now well known for my questioning approach to resolving issues!'

Another had found that everything in the company seemed connected:

'I started off trying to introduce some rationality into the queueing system for orders, but as I progressed through the company – with a lot of encouragement from my boss and from the MD – I realised that what was wrong was the whole way we were organised. In the terms I've learned since being here, we needed to be less of a hierarchy and more of a lateral flow from buyer to supplier and back to buyer. So what we have is a major change instead of a minor one – much of it is

being done by other people of course – but it's been very exciting being the cause of it all.'

The crucial role of top management was clear in another account:

'The biggest theme for me is the impact of top managers. If the person at the top is learning something new for themselves, then the whole organisation is healthier. Sadly, it seems to me that the evidence from this project is more negative than positive. Top managers seem to be lonely figures, struggling with huge agendas, often continuing to get involved in day-to-day operational issues, anxious and stressed about personal futures and not appearing to be using personal support or learning processes to any great extent.'

Quite often learning is about the learning process itself:

'There is a sudden moment when learning happens... I had been in turmoil... unable to come to terms with the problem facing me. I didn't want the change and I couldn't talk to anybody... I was under stress – being disagreeable, wallowing in self-pity, arguing the toss with myself. I decided to speak to the one person who could help and woke up that morning thinking "this is

Action Learning in practice". Of course, that person couldn't help me, but the conversation wasn't futile because I suddenly realised that this was my problem – that only I could do something about it. This seems to me to be the quintessential moment – when you decide to own the problem and not make it someone else's fault that you have the problem.'

and…

'We didn't all learn the same things or at the same time – the penny dropped for us at different times – and some people learned more and others seemed to benefit less..'

One person had adopted the Action Learning approach in many aspects of her life:

'Action Learning has become more like a philosophy to me, something I use in all my activities. I challenge myself all the time, Why? For what reason? Be positive! There is an answer! I have also suffered pain, emotionally, going through change myself with the organisation. We cannot be divorced from it, if we affect it, it must affect us, touch us.'

Whilst these skills, abilities and qualities will help people to action and learning, they are not the most important part of Action Learning. Skilled performance is almost always to be preferred to unskilled, but the first principle in Action Learning remains the desire and willingness to learn and act.

If you're learning you can't be skilled all the time – being incompetent at times is part of the process. So you don't need all these skills to get started on Action Learning. The most important question remains: 'Are you willing to give it a go?'.

The **resource** below gives some useful ideas for questioning – the first and primary skill of Action Learning:

Good questions for Action Learning

Revans' three key questions:

1 *Who knows...* about the problem?

2 *Who cares...* about the problem?... and...

3 *Who can...* do anything about the problem?

These questions are more than enough to get started, referring as they do to the crucial processes in human action – thinking, feeling and willing. Much management education concentrates upon just one of these processes: thinking – Do you understand the problem? Have you analysed it correctly? But, how you *feel* about the situation you're in and how much commitment or *will* you have for action, are just as important. Well-educated people in particular may be at risk of getting stuck at the thinking stage where planning never leads to action. Useful questions for action and learning are:

- What am I trying to do?

- What is stopping me from doing it?

- What can I do about it?

- Who knows what I am trying to do?

- Who cares about what I'm trying to do?

- Who else can do anything to help?

Here are some other questions which may facilitate work in the set:

- What do you want to get out of this session?

- Can you tell us the story as it happened?

- What have you learned from that?

- What do you most need from us now?

- How do other people in the situation – colleagues,

friends, partner, boss etc feel about this?

- How do you feel about what is going on?

- What questions does that raise?

- How can we help someone move forwards on their issue?

- How would someone you most admire deal with this situation?

- Can you think of three options for action?

- What are the pros and cons of each of thee options?

- What first steps are you going to take before our next meeting?

- How can we make this set more effective?

These sort of questions are often modelled by the set adviser or facilitator – but that person does not have a monopoly of this skill. You can have a go at Action Learning without an outside facilitator. It is possible for sets to be self-facilitating where members take on the role in turn or where they try to carry it collectively. (See Ian McGill and Liz Beaty's book listed in chapter 9). This is not to say that set advisers are not helpful. Many people would say that, most of the time, they are essential, especially in the early stages. As the case study of John Tann (chapter 2) showed, the lack of an outside person was seen as the main reason why Action Learning failed to continue.

One question which is always raised about Action Learning concerns evaluation. How do we know that it is worthwhile?

7 How do you evaluate Action Learning?

To evaluate means to place a value upon something against certain criteria. The more specific these criteria are, the easier it is to determine value, and it is good practice to encourage people to think about what the 'success criteria' are for their participation in the Action Learning programme.

You can evaluate for two purposes, for...

1 **development** – to make things better, to improve action and learning

or for...

2 **judgment** – to assess the impact or contribution of something.

Developmental evaluation ought to be part of the on-going life of any set, and the **resource** in this chapter provides a simple form for reviewing a set meeting for the purpose of improving action and learning.

Judgmental evaluation is important to establish whether goals have been met and resources well used. Where specific criteria can be set, results can be compared against the targets.

Although evaluation is a critical activity and should be planned in from the outset, it can be a struggle to keep it simple and efficient. It is easy to get sucked into massive efforts at data collection, because the task of estimating the worth or value of something is often a difficult one. How is it possible to disentangle the actions of this person, or group, from everything else which is happening? It is easiest to assess the effects of something close up: 'the set seemed to work well today' or 'I learned so much this morning', but what is the ultimate value of the action and learning?

To answer this question you have to look at the effects on tasks and ultimately on the company as a whole. The work of a set can be evaluated at several levels:

- *individual* – in terms of progress on a problem and learning from it
- *set* – in terms of collective achievement and group development and maturity
- *programme or whole company level* – across the sets, the impact on an organisation as a whole.

You can also evaluate at different points in time, for example:

- *immediate outcome* – e.g. at the end of set meeting (see **resource** below)
- *intermediate outcome* – e.g. half way through a programme
- *programme outcome* – at the end of the programme
- *organisational outcome* – long enough after the programme to gauge the effects on the company.

As you get to the whole company level, in terms of judgmental evaluation, it is difficult to ascribe cause and effect. How do we know that the Action Learning programme reduced costs by 23 per cent – when there were so many other factors at work? Often, the best we can do here is to get people's opinions on the likely causes of such changes. In the case of qualitative data, such as opinions, it is useful to collect it from all the main stakeholders to a given problem.

The **case example** below gives a method for identifying stakeholders and their success criteria for an Action Learning programme in schools:

An Action Learning set for headteachers and deputies

An Action Learning set of headteachers and deputies identified some internal and external stakeholders for their schools:

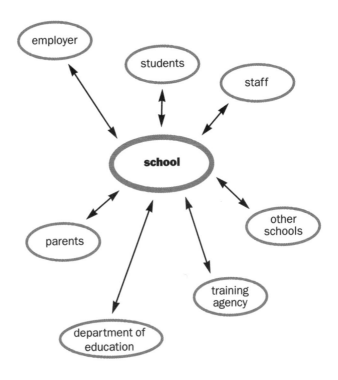

Each person used the stakeholder map to identify the critical success criteria for their projects. For example, one deputy was concerned to improve the delivery of various aspects of the National Curriculum in the school:

Stakeholder	Success criteria	Evidence needed
Students	i 'more interesting lessons' ii 'to know what is expected in terms of assessment' – and so on	i End of term lesson reviews ii Improved achievements
Parents	i 'to know how their child is doing' open evenings ii 'to know how to help their child do well' – and so on	i Feedback on reports and ii Access to after-school information sessions – and so on
Department of Education		

At the end of the programme the set carried out a rigorous evaluation, visiting each other's schools to help check progress in terms of how far stakeholder criteria had been met In terms of the benefits to individuals and their schools. A report noted various examples:

■ Staff in one school reported that 'Relationships between the school and parents have improved dramatically. Attendances at Open Evenings have doubled and parents report feeling more confident in terms of asking for information.'

■ A headteacher said 'It helped me a lot. I used to get very stressed and had a bad relationship with my deputy. Now our ability to communicate and work together has improved. I feel better and I think the school does too.'

■ Several set members said they had picked up all sorts of tools and techniques from other members which they had put into practice in their schools.

■ A Chairman of Governors interviewed by two members of the set said that she and the other governors had noticed the school seemed 'to be running more smoothly and that there was less of an air of crisis.'

- Various improvements in performance and achievements were observed in the schools.

- One deputy said 'It was an oasis... sheer bliss to get away from the school for half a day and have people actually listen to you! Also to listen to yourself... and to hear how other people were tackling their problems.'

Self-evaluation is an important part of Action Learning. Self-awareness and improving one's ability to self-evaluate can be an important outcome in itself.

Carrying out a more formal judgmental evaluation, for example, interviewing stakeholders and assessing how far their expectations have been met can be a good last task for an Action Learning set. As a collective review of their work and learning it can be an excellent way to 'make a good end'.

A minimum specification for evaluation is twofold:

1 A regular review and developmental evaluation in set meetings and...

2 A summary judgmental evaluation of the worth of the programme as a whole to the individuals and the

organisation concerned.

Finally the **resource** for this chapter is a Set Meeting Review Worksheet which is useful, especially in the early stages of a set, to embed the evaluation habit:

Set Meeting Review Worksheet

Each person should spend five minutes reflecting individually on the work of the set and before sharing with fellow members.

My problem

The three key things I have learned about my problem today are...

1 _____

_____

_____

2 _____

_____

_____

3 _____

_____

_____

Myself

The one thing I've learned about myself today is...

_____

_____

_____

Action

My action steps before the next meeting are...

_____

_____

_____

_____

_____

_____

Other set members

The most interesting thing I have learned today about the problems facing each of the other set members is...

Name

_____

_____

_____

Name

Name

Name

The set

The thing that stands out for me today in terms of the working of this set is...

_____

_____

_____

_____

_____

Through Action Learning we can achieve some impressive results – for both the individual and the organisation. Having said that, it is important to bear in mind that this is no panacea, no miracle cure. I have tried to point out some likely pitfalls throughout, whilst at the same time trying to encourage you to get on with it. Please do this, and then read chapter 8 when you're ready to reflect on the method itself.

8 Surely Action Learning can't do everything?

No, of course it can't. Some of the chief limitations of Action Learning have been spelled out earlier, especially in chapter 2. Conditions have to be right for Action Learning, there has to be a readiness – in individuals and in companies – or it will not take hold. In all the Action Learning programmes I've worked on, some sets have worked better than others; some people have got a great deal from the process whilst others – usually a small minority – find that it didn't work for them.

If your purpose is to train individuals in specific skills or knowledge, then there are probably more efficient and effective methods than Action Learning. If your purpose is to transform an organisation then Action Learning can certainly play a part in helping people to contribute to and adjust to this process. But something more than this process is probably required including vision, leadership and will from the top, massive resource commitment and so on.

Yet Action Learning is not simply an alternative educational or training method, nor is it just DIY consultancy, problem-solving or project management – though it can make a contribution to all these things. It is first and foremost an educational idea or philosophy, aimed at healing the split which Revans saw as having developed historically between thinking and doing, between ideas and action. In presenting action and learning as parts of each other, he aimed to contribute to more effective action on the many urgent and pressing problems facing our society. In particular he was concerned about those not able to help themselves – which includes all of us from time to time – but some of us most of the time. He has described the essence of Action Learning as 'helping each other to help the helpless'.

Revans is a radical and it is clear from his writings that he intends Action Learning to be a deeper, more revolutionary process than just a training method for 'learning by doing'. Action Learning, being about individual and organisational development, contains a *moral philosophy* involving:

● **honesty about self** – the most valuable question learned by the top managers on his Belgian programme was 'What is an honest man, and what do I need to do to become one?'

● **attempting to do good in the world** – Revans' quotes both St James: 'Be ye doers of the Word, and not only hearers of it.', and Shaw's echo in *Back to Methuselah*: 'It is not enough to know what is good; you must be able to do it.'

● **for the purpose of friendship** – 'All meaningful knowledge is for the sake of action, and all meaningful action is for the sake of friendship.' (John Macmurray's *The Self as Agent* – a key text for Revans.)

Without selling this philosophy short, many people all over the world have learned the value of Action Learning without ever having heard of Revans, and without reading his books. This is because Action Learning provides a practical form of managerial self-help which fits many of the needs of our times. As one manager put it:

> 'the group format provides rare 'space' in organisational life; a time for reflection and review; a way of linking individual and collective learning; permission to be completely open in a confidential setting; and support, challenge and encouragement. These features allow learning both about management and, at a deeper level, about oneself as a manager.'

The **case example** illustrates the practical value of Action Learning through the work of Tony, a hospital doctor, who is angry about his organisation and who wants to change things. As well as being angry, he feels powerless, impotent...

An angry doctor

Tony is a psychiatrist in a large NHS Community Trust. He is angry a lot of the time – angry about the changes to the Health Service, the pressures on him, the service offered to his patients, the attitude of managers who always seem to want more for less and offer little in the way of help. There's a lot to be angry about. Yet this anger actually doesn't help him to get what he wants.

The adviser stops Tony in the middle of one of his rants and suggests that he take ten or fifteen minutes to draw the situation as he experiences it. After a short argument, Tony goes off with a pen and a flipchart to another room. He returns with the picture shown over the page:

The dilemma of the doctor and the manager

The adviser asks Tony...

'How does it feel for each of the people in the picture?'

... which leads to an interesting discussion about the feelings of the manager in the picture. The adviser then puts two more questions and a proposal to Tony in the next 20 minutes of discussion...

'What does the picture tell us about the relationship?'

(The most obvious thing which emerges here – obvious to one set member – is that that the two have their backs to each other...)

'What is stopping movement on this problem?'

... and...

'Tony, can you come back next time having given some thought to the 'I – we – they' actions...

- *What do I need to do?...*

- *What do we need to do?... and...*

- *What do they need to do?... (that is, those people not in the picture).*

Is that OK?'

Tony agrees to go and think about these questions, talk to a few people and report back next time.

By breaking out of words for a time, the adviser gets Tony to look at himself with a bit more clarity and perhaps a bit more honesty about his own contribution to the situation. This does not mean that Tony is wrong to be angry. Quite the contrary – anger is a sound feeling in the face of injustice and unfairness, but it can be a bad master when it comes to action. The concern is for action and learning possibilities which might make things more healthy.

This **case example** shows how drawing problems in their organisational context can help the people in that situation get a clearer perspective. Professionals and managers deal in words, and we can often get lost in them. Sometimes we use them as a screen to hide behind. It becomes such second nature that we don't even know we are doing it ourselves. Getting away from words can move us a little nearer to clarity, honesty, and openness. Drawing the situation is one way of doing this.

Although Revans is always on the side of the individual seeking to act and learn, he is also concerned to specify the conditions which organisations should establish to promote Action Learning. These amount to his vision about how to go about creating the Learning Company:

Revans on the Learning Company

Reg Revans has always made it clear that Action Learning is not just about individual learning in small groups. His 'upward communication of doubt' is perhaps the briefest description for the Learning Company. In his 1969 paper 'The Enterprise as a Learning System' he outlines the conditions for this to be achieved:

■ 'that its chief executive places high amongst his own responsibilities developing the enterprise as a learning system; this he will achieve through his personal relations with his immediate subordinates, since the conduct of one level of a system towards any level below it is powerfully influenced by the perception that the higher level has of its own treatment from above…

■ … the maximum authority for subordinates to act… *become known by interrogation from below…*

■ … codes of practice, standard rules and procedures, works orders and other such regulations are to be seen as norms around which variations are deliberately encouraged as learning opportunities...

■ any reference to what appears to be an intractable problem to a superior level should be accompanied by *both* an explanation of why it cannot be treated where it seems to have arisen *and* a proposal to change the system so that similar problems arising in future could be suitably contained and treated

■ persons at all levels should be encouraged, with their immediate colleagues, to make regular proposals for the study and reorganisation of their own systems of work.'

R W Revans, 'The Enterprise as a Learning System' in The Origins and Growth of Action Learning *(Chartwell-Bratt, 1982) , re-printed in M Pedler* Action Learning in Practice *2nd ed. (Gower, 1991).*

⑨ Where can I get more help?

As you've no doubt gathered by now, there's really only only way to get going with Action Learning, and that is to try it. If you've read this far then you're interested enough to have a go – take some (sober and deliberate) action and you will learn.

Some final advice:

- *Don't* try to structure up the Action Learning programme too much.
- *Don't* control the life out of the idea… and, especially…
- *Don't* follow all of the advice in this guide!

However, it will help if you…

- *Do* recruit some interested friends and allies to work with you on it.

- *Do* choose some of the interesting and intractable problems around you to work with.

- *Do* make the time to reflect and learn on your actions, keep a journal, and carry out your evaluations.

There is an active network of people involved in Action Learning and you might want to get in touch with this. The details are given below. If you want to read more and you can trust yourself not to let reading substitute for Action Learning, here also are some useful books.

People and organisations

An international network of people involved in Action Learning is:

IFAL (The International Foundation for Action Learning) is a registered educational charity. IFAL maintains a library, a bibliographic service, holds workshops, provides an advisory service, publishes a newsletter and otherwise disseminates information about Action Learning. The IFAL library alone contains some 800 items and a full list is available. Membership is open to individuals and organisations. Details are obtainable from the secretary, Krystyna Weinstein at:

IFAL
46 Carlton Road
London SW14 7RJ

Telephone and fax 0181 878 7358

The Learning Company Project is based on a partnership of Tom Boydell, John Burgoyne and Mike Pedler and conducts research, development and consultancy assignments in various aspects of organisational learning. It also holds conferences and manages consortia in the UK and USA. Further information may be had from the LCP's manager, Gloria Welshman at:

Learning Company Project
28 Woodholm Road
Sheffield S11 9HT

Telephone and fax 0114 262 1832

Books

Reg Revans has written eloquently over many years about Action Learning. His books repay repeated study. Unfortunately most of these are now out of print but may be found in libraries, including IFAL's. These books include:

The ABC of Action Learning (Chartwell-Bratt, Bromley, Kent, 1983) (His shortest at 84 pages but solidly packed; in effect the 'authorised version').

The Origins and Growth of Action Learning (Chartwell-Bratt, Bromley, Kent, 1982) (The 'collected works' – over 50 papers from 1945 to 1981).

Developing Effective Managers (Praeger, New York, 1971) (A significant development of Action Learning ideas based on a Belgian programme which swapped top managers between industries).

Other books on Action Learning

Mike Pedler (Ed.) *Action Learning in Practice* 2nd ed. (Gower, Aldershot, 1991) (A worldwide review of Action Learning practice with contributions from many of the leading practitioners. Contains a bibliography and a list of practitioners).

Ian McGill and Liz Beaty *Action Learning: A Practitioner's Guide* (Kogan Page, London, 1992) (A useful book which is particularly good on the skills involved and also contains advice on how to run your own set without a facilitator).

Krystyna Weinstein *Action Learning: A journey in discovery and development* (HarperCollins, London, 1995) (Good, easy read, distinguished by its giving voice to many participants in Action Learning sets).

David Casey and David Pearce (Eds) *More than
Management Development: Action Learning at GEC*
(Gower, Aldershot, 1977) (An account of a major
programme of Action Learning at GEC).

Articles on Action Learning

Alan Mumford 'Learning in Action', *Personnel
Management* (July 1991) pp34–37 (A practitioner offers
his own interpretation of Action Learning ideas).

Liz Beaty, Tom Bourner and Paul Frost 'Action
Learning: Reflections on becoming a set member',
Management Education & Development 24(4) (1993)
(Experiences of self-facilitated Action Learning).

Books on the wider implications of Action Learning

Mike Pedler, John Burgoyne and Tom Boydell
A Manager's Guide to Self-development 3rd ed.
(McGraw-Hill, Maidenhead, 1994) (A comprehensive

guide to management self-development – friendly, challenging and action learning oriented).

Mike Pedler and Tom Boydell *Managing Yourself* 2nd ed. (Fontana/HarperCollins, London, 1994) (Includes a model of the manager as a person with ideas and methods for self-development).

Mike Pedler, John Burgoyne and Tom Boydell *The Learning Company* (McGraw-Hill, Maidenhead, June 1991) (Contains the eleven characteristics of the learning company and the energy flow model together with 101 glimpses of the learning company in action).

David Casey *Managing Learning in Organisations* (Open University Press, Milton Keynes, 1993) (Includes Action Learning as a main perspective but includes chapters on working with teams, Chief Executives and the whole organisation).

Nancy Dixon *The Organisational Learning Cycle* (McGraw-Hill, Maidenhead, 1994) (From an author who has pioneered the use of action learning in the USA, a book on how an organisational learning cycle parallels the individual cycle).

Ian Cunningham *The Wisdom of Strategic Learning* (McGraw-Hill, Maidenhead, 1994) (This book uses the idea of self-managed learning to look at how to bring about the 'Learning Business').

Mike Pedler and Kath Aspinwall *'Perfect Plc?': The purpose and practice of organisational learning* (McGraw-Hill, Maidenhead, 1996) (This book contains a wide variety of case examples of the learning company in practice and also asks the question 'What is all this learning for?').

Index